"Let the word of Christ dwell in you richly, teaching and admonishing one another in all wisdom, singing psalms and hymns and spiritual songs, with thankfulness in your hearts to God" (Colossians 3:16).

Whether we're writing songs, planning worship, or just fellowshipping together, Colossians 3:16 is never far from our minds. It's a beautiful description of a church that is saturated with the gospel. We want this collection of meditations to help the word of Christ dwell richly in you. For that to happen, we urge you to read the passages recommended at the beginning of each devotional. If this or any other Christian book replaces the Bible rather than driving you further into it, it will harm you, not help you. Dig into the God-breathed, life-changing Scriptures.

On the other hand, Colossians 3:16 does commend our "teaching and admonishing" each other with the word of Christ. With that in mind, we're glad to publish this booklet as a small part of that Christian-to-Christian instruction. We've done our best with both this book and its counterpart, *Gospel Meditations for Women*, to write expositional studies that reflect the context of the Scriptures they address. We pray that you'll grow in your appreciation and application of the gospel as you study them. And we're hopeful it won't stop with you. Though the word of Christ should be "at home" in your life, it shouldn't stay there. It should burst forth in praising God (exaltation), reaching the lost (evangelism), and serving the body of Christ (edification). Don't just take in the truth from these pages—do something with it!

We dedicate *Gospel Meditations for Men* to our fathers, Chuck Anderson and Peter Tyrpak. Both of them have consistently demonstrated to us what a life overflowing with gospel truth looks like. We'd also like to thank the members of Tri-County Bible Church, where we're privileged to labor together and pastor each other. It's at Tri-County where these truths were first preached. Because we love Christ, we love His church! We're grateful to our fellow elders at Tri-County—Johnny, Mark, and Kris—with whom we've discussed and prayed over many of these lessons. Finally, many thanks to Abby Huffstutler and Greg Buchanan, who assisted us with meticulous editing. You're brutal—in a good way!

May the Lord use this resource for the good of the church, the advancement of the gospel, and the praise of His glory (Ephesians 1:12).

For the sake of His name,

Chris Anderson & Joe Tyrpak

His Robes for Mine

READ ISAIAH 53 & 61:10

For our sake he made him to be sin who knew no sin,
so that in him we might become the righteousness of God.

2 CORINTHIANS 5:21

In Mark Twain's implausible but entertaining novel *The Prince and the Pauper*, two boys—identical in appearance, but opposites in social standing—trade positions and experiences by trading clothes. The prince longs for freedom from court life, so he put on the rags of a guttersnipe. The pauper yearns for the comforts of the palace, so he dons the robes of royalty. The story aptly illustrates the biblical doctrine of imputation which is essential to getting the gospel right. The boys were treated either well or ill entirely on the basis of their assumed identities. So it is for those who repent of their sins and trust in Jesus Christ as their only hope of salvation. God has made a "great exchange" in which His Son was treated like a sinner and repentant sinners are treated like His Son (2 Corinthians 5:21).

God clothed Jesus in our sins. The Father "made [Jesus] to be sin" (2 Corinthians 5:21a). The eternal Son of God "knew no sin"—He is the only person who has ever lived a sinless life (1 Peter 2:22). We, in stark contrast, are so morally polluted with the mire of sin that even our *best* acts are filthy rags (Isaiah 64:6). Yet, in great love for sinners and obedience to His Father's will, the sinless Savior donned the rags of the wicked. "He bore our sins in His body on the tree" (1 Peter 2:24). On the cross, Jesus was clothed in our rebellion, our lust, our deception. Even more astoundingly, He was punished by His Father as though He Himself were guilty of those sins. God forsook and crushed His Son (Matthew 27:46; Isaiah 53:4-6, 10). Jesus, draped in our sin, absorbed all of the wrath which our sin incurred. God's wrath was satisfied, and God's justice was appeased by the death of His own Son (1 John 2:1-2).

God clothes repentant sinners in the righteousness of Jesus Christ. Beyond counting our sins against His Son, God completed the great exchange by crediting Jesus' obedience to us: "that in him we might become the righteousness of God" (2 Corinthians 5:21b). Just as God treated heaven's Prince as though He were an enemy, so God also credits the righteousness of Christ to rebellious sinners and treats us as though we were sinless princes. This is the genius of the Bible doctrine of justification (Romans 3:21-26). All who trust in Christ are clothed in a righteousness that is *not our own* (what theologians rightly call an "alien righteousness"), the very righteousness Christ earned by His perfect obedience to the Father while He lived on earth (Philippians 3:9-10; Isaiah 61:10). In this divine version of *The Prince and the Pauper*, God has treated Christ and sinners not according to their actual identities but according to their exchanged robes and assumed roles. Christ was punished, the sinner pardoned. Christ was banished, the sinner welcomed. Christ was cursed, the sinner blessed. This is our only hope. Marvel at it. Respond to it by trusting Christ as your only Savior and treasuring Him as your greatest Joy.

His robes for mine: such anguish none can know.
Christ, God's beloved, condemned as though His foe.
He, as though I, accursed and left alone;
I, as though He, embraced and welcomed home!

Let the gospel provide the righteousness you lack. —CHRIS

Creation & New Creation

READ GENESIS 1

*For God, who said, "Let light shine out of darkness,"
has shone in our hearts.*

2 CORINTHIANS 4:6

he way God created the world parallels the way the gospel affects the hearts of sinners
2 Corinthians 4:6). So when we read the first chapter of Genesis, we should marvel at
;od's power to form the world with the word of His mouth; then we should let that
eepen our confidence in God's power to transform people with the word of the cross.
;enesis 1 reveals three ways in which God created the universe, all of which build our
onfidence in the gospel.

;od creates with His powerful word. Every one of the six days of creation opens with
ie words, "And God said." God created the universe with nothing but His speech.
.onsider the power involved in that! A potter uses a wheel, clay, water, and his fingers.
. carpenter uses wood, nails, hammers, and his biceps. God, however, used nothing but
iis own breath to create everything that exists. Compare the power of God's word with
our own. When you speak, how many listen? How many care? How many change?
f you're like me, you probably have difficulty getting even your own children to pay
ttention to what you say. But when God speaks, the universe comes into existence!
his awesome power of God's word is talked about throughout the rest of the Bible.
The word of God is living and active" (Hebrews 4:12). "All Scripture is breathed out
y God and profitable"—even capable of saving and sanctifying sinners (2 Timothy
:15-17; see 1 Peter 1:23). As God's word was creatively powerful during the first six
ays of creation, so the gospel of Christ has the power to create life in the soul.

;od creates by His Holy Spirit. "The Spirit of God was hovering over the face of the
aters" (Genesis 1:2)—this means that the Spirit was poised and ready to carry out
hatever God commanded. It's as if the hovering Spirit is a zealous soldier that's pulsing
ith excitement as he eagerly anticipates the order from his commander's lips. As soon
s he hears the word, he's ready to rush into action. Throughout the six days of creation,
;od spoke the word, and the Spirit executed it (see Psalm 104:30). Again, this reveals
omething significant about God's mode of operation. As in creation, so in conversion:
;od wills it, and the Spirit works it. When we hear the message of the gospel, God's
pirit is the One who convicts us, opens our eyes, gives us life, unites us with Christ,
ndwells us, and forever seals us as God's possession.

;od creates order from chaos. Have you ever wondered why we're told at the outset
f the week of creation that the earth was "without form and void, and [covered in]
larkness" (Genesis 1:2)? It's as if God draws back the curtain and lets us come "behind
he scenes" and see how His initial creation of space and matter looked before He
tarted forming it. God gives us this "backstage tour" because He wants us to know that
iis creative word always brings order out of disorder, that His creation always moves in
he direction of beauty and completeness. After six days of creating, speaking, dividing,
etting boundaries, and assigning names and purposes, "everything that He had made...
vas very good" (1:31).

;od can bring beautiful order out of a ruined mess. Have you lost confidence in
he power of the gospel? Do you feel empty and dark on the inside? What God did
osmically, He still does personally—through His Spirit-empowered word.

_et the gospel's power encourage you today. —JOE

Your Spiritual Self-Identity
READ 1 TIMOTHY 1

The saying is trustworthy and deserving of full acceptance,
that Christ Jesus came into the world to save sinners,
of whom I am the foremost.

1 TIMOTHY 1:15

Men often define themselves by such things as politics, sports teams, and careers. But I'd like to ask you to define yourself *spiritually*. What is your spiritual self-identity? Ar you an orthodox guy? A conservative guy? A family guy? A good guy? I suggest that t most obvious self-description of a Christian man—the one that pops most readily int your head—should be this: *"I'm a sinner in need of God's grace. I'm a mess, and I need Jesus."* 1 Timothy 1:15 should be your calling card, leading to two basic admissions.

"I'm a rebellious and undeserving sinner." Paul describes himself in 1 Timothy 1:1 as the foremost of sinners—the "chief," as the KJV says. He was ever mindful of his past as a blasphemer of God, a persecutor of Christ's church, and a violent opponent God's work (1 Timothy 1:13; Acts 22:4; 26:9-11; 1 Corinthians 15:9; Galatians 1:13 Ephesians 3:8; Philippians 3:6). And, in addition to remembering his past offenses, Paul uses a present tense verb ("I *am* the foremost") to claim that he was *still* the chief of sinners, even as a Christian.

Some suggest that Paul's statement was strictly factual: that Saul of Tarsus (Paul, B.C.) was the worst sinner to ever walk the planet. That's saying a lot, both in light of histor and with an eye on the many "depravity lists" Paul penned in the Scriptures (Romans 1:28-32; Galatians 5:24-25; 2 Timothy 3:1-9). Indeed, in 1 Timothy 1:9-10, just a few verses before his claim to be the worst (best?) sinner ever, Paul describes sinners as "lawless, disobedient, ungodly, unholy, and profane." He specifically mentions parent abusers, murderers, fornicators, homosexuals, slave traders, liars, and perjurers. That's quite a list! Was Paul really a worse sinner than everyone else? Well, I tend to think he reflecting a Christian's awareness of guilt rather than making an absolute claim. It's as he's saying, "Whatever anyone else has done, I know my own heart, and I'm the wors sinner I know." I think it's a self-assessment that I should share: *I'm* the chief of sinner I'm more scandalized by what I see in myself than what I see in anyone else. And *you* should see yourself as the chief of sinners. That should be *your* self-identity.

"I'm a recipient of gospel grace through Jesus Christ." The point of 1 Timothy 1:15 isn't that you should wallow in self-condemnation. Paul highlights his own sin specifically to magnify Jesus' astounding power to save. What Paul is teaching about *Christ* is the point he describes as "trustworthy and deserving of all acceptance" (Paul' way of using bold, italicized caps): "Christ Jesus came into the world to save sinners." He came to earth on a rescue mission, and He succeeded. That's why Paul so often rehearses the fact that Jesus endured the wrath of God which our sin has earned (Romans 3:25; 5:8; 1 Corinthians 15:3). Paul knew that he was saved in spite of himself. That's the point of the entire passage that surrounds our text (1 Timothy 1:1 17)—that every saved sinner is a trophy of God's grace!

In the shadow of the cross you'll see yourself as no better than any other sinner. Your wonder at your depravity and at Jesus' saving grace will never diminish. On your *best* day and *worst* day, you'll define yourself as a sinner saved by grace, all to Jesus' glory.

Let the gospel make you more aware of your own sin than anyone else's, and more aware of God's grace than either. —CHRIS

A Psalm for Life

READ PSALM 23 & JOHN 10

The LORD is my shepherd; I shall not want.

PSALM 23:1

You're watching a movie in which someone dies. The scene fades from the quiet hospital room to a somber cemetery. It's raining—every time. Everyone's wearing black clothing and standing under black umbrellas. As soon as the sound becomes audible, what do you hear? The minister reading Scripture—and nine times out of ten, it's Psalm 23: "The Lord is my shepherd; I shall not want." In our culture, Psalm 23 is the stereotypical funeral text. And Psalm 23 certainly provides comfort for dying Christians and for Christians who have lost a loved one. But the twenty-third Psalm wasn't written for funerals; it was written to provide comfort *for life*! It was intended for living, breathing men who are feeling threatened and helpless. It was penned by a man—a godly, masculine, exemplary king—to calm his fearful heart. What should you do when you're afraid, when you're going "through the valley of the shadow of death," when you're standing "in the presence of [your] enemies" (23:4-5)? You should sing Psalm 23: "The LORD is my shepherd; I have everything I need" (NLT).

What does your Shepherd do? First, He *revives* you (23:2-3a). In times of trial when you're hungry and tired, the Lord renews your strength by giving you the rest and food you need—both physically and spiritually. Second, He *leads* you (23:3b). You can be certain that your Shepherd will keep you from straying off the right path, because His name is at stake—His reputation is on the line (Isaiah 48:11). Third, the Lord *comforts* you with His presence (23:4). When you're going through the darkest times of your life, your Shepherd is there with you. You'll know His presence by how He defends you with His rod and disciplines you with His staff (Derek Kidner, *Psalms 1-72*, p. 111). Fourth, your Shepherd *blesses* you (23:5-6). His blessings will overflow even as you're surrounded by enemies, and His covenant love will continually "hunt you down" until the day you're with Him forever. Your Shepherd revives you, leads you, comforts you, and blesses you. Sing from your heart, "The LORD is my Shepherd; I have everything I need."

Who is your Shepherd? *The Lord* is your Shepherd. The God that created the heavens and the earth, the "I Am" that parted the Red Sea, the Commander that crumbled the walls of Jericho—He is your Shepherd. *The Lord Jesus* is your Shepherd. When Jesus said, "I am the good shepherd" (John 10:11), He was making an audacious claim. Many thought that He was "insane" (10:20) because He was saying in essence, "I am Jehovah, the Shepherd of Psalm 23." He followed that with a statement that was just as baffling: "The good shepherd lays down his life for the sheep" (10:11). That's like saying, "The farmer's going to die for his cows." Unthinkable! That's a level of care and concern that no shepherd has ever had. You say, "But the shepherd ceases to look like a shepherd and starts to look like a sacrificial lamb." Precisely. *The Lamb* is your Shepherd. For all eternity, "the Lamb in the midst of the throne will be [your] shepherd" (Revelation 7:17). "The Lord is my Shepherd; I have everything I need."

Perhaps you've never noticed, but Psalm 23 doesn't command you to do anything. Why? Because you can't do one thing to make the Lord Jesus Christ a better Shepherd for you. You can't make Him love you more or protect you more than He does. Throughout all the trials and fears of your life, all you can do is rest in the care of your Good Shepherd.

Let the gospel calm your fears. —JOE

The Basis for True Humility
READ ISAIAH 6

Woe is me! For I am lost...
for my eyes have seen the King, the LORD of hosts.
ISAIAH 6:5

Humans—and perhaps men in particular—are nothing if not proud. We love ourselves, promote ourselves, and defend ourselves. Arrogance is sewn into our fallen nature. The problem is this: God detests pride. Proverbs 16:5 says that the proud *person* (not just pride as an impersonal concept) is an abomination to God. James 4:6 teaches that God actively opposes the proud. Pride is dangerous and foolish. Spurgeon described pride as "a groundless thing" and "a brainless thing" and "the maddest thing that can exist" (in a sermon preached on August 17, 1856).

How, then, can we cultivate humility? Is it a way of walking or speaking? Is it an *"Aw, shucks"* personality? A self-loathing? On what is true humility based? Scripture answers these questions definitively in Isaiah 6:1-7. True humility begins with a right estimation of God.

Our humility grows when we recognize God's unrivaled majesty. The prophet Isaiah was given the unfathomable privilege of seeing God's majesty (6:1)—the glory of the pre-incarnate Christ, according to John 12:41! Jehovah was enthroned in the temple, which shook beneath His sovereignty (6:1, 4). His robe had a vast train which testified of His splendor (6:1). He was identified as "the King" and "the Lord of hosts" (think "Commander in Chief," 6:5). His reign outshone the recently ended reign of King Uzziah (6:1). Whereas Uzziah had died, Jehovah lives. Whereas Uzziah's reign was limited in time and sphere, Jehovah's is infinite. There is no King like Christ. We too would be humbled if we would see God in all of His majesty.

Our humility grows when we recognize God's unrivaled glory. Verses 2-4 go on to describe angelic worship in God's presence. Seraphim surround the throne of God and call out His praises. They've done so since their creation, are doing so today, and will continue to do so for eternity. Their flying signifies service. Their covering of their faces and feet shows reverence and humility, which is astounding. As magnificent as the seraphim are—and their very title means "fiery ones"—they're *still* humbled before God. He alone is "Holy, holy, holy" (6:3); He is completely unique; no one is like Him. Even sinless angels have no grounds for boasting before their matchless Creator. We too would be humbled if we would see God in all of His glory.

Our humility grows when we recognize God's unrivaled purity. Finally, in Isaiah 6:5, the prophet responded to what he had seen by acknowledging his own sinfulness. Although he lived in a notoriously wicked nation (as he testified throughout the book), he didn't presume to side with God in condemning sinners "out there." Rather, he saw himself as a part of the sin problem all around him. He needed cleansing, which God mercifully granted (6:6-7). Isaiah, one of the godliest men of history, needed the forgiveness provided by the ultimate altar, the cross of Christ (Hebrews 10:10, 14). We too would be humbled if we would see God in all of His purity.

True humility is rooted in the gospel. We find it in studying Christ through the Scriptures and responding to Him with faith, love, and worship. My friend Tim Potter puts it this way: "Humility is constantly measuring ourselves by God." Bow to Jesus, and watch the gospel remove your pride even as it reveals it.

Let the Gospel crush your pride. —CHRIS

Battling Lust

READ PROVERBS 5, 7 & 9

For a man's ways are before the eyes of the Lord,
and he ponders all his paths.

PROVERBS 5:21

Here's a comical statistic: "95% of men struggle with lust; the other 5% struggle with lying." What's *not* funny is the reality that every man struggles with lust. Thankfully, the Scripture doesn't blink or blush when addressing the problem of sexual lust. Nowhere is the Bible's teaching on the battle against lust more dense than in Proverbs 5-9. Unpacking those proverbs would require more space than we have, but after you've read them, consider some basic lessons that will help in your battle against lust.

Avoid tempting circumstances. The simpleton in Proverbs 7 is either dangerously naïve or brazenly bold. He's in the wrong place at the wrong time (7:6-9), possibly for the thrill of courting temptation. You've probably been there. Proverbs 5:8 warns us to steer clear of temptation, when possible. Stay away from tempting places (a particular store?), circumstances (staying up alone at night?), and people (an attractive lady at work?).

Eliminate anonymity and establish accountability. Part of the simpleton's problem is that he's alone. Such solitude is even more dangerous today with the lure of online pornography. Men who would be terrified to enter an adult bookstore or gentlemen's club (both of which are grossly misnamed) can surf the web in relative secrecy. If you're serious about purity, eliminate such anonymity. Don't try to battle your lust alone. Pursue discipleship with trustworthy Christian men, ideally your own church leaders. Ask for prayer. Get accountability software. Be transparent. Lust is an "in the dark" sin that is best fought in the light of responsible Christian fellowship (Galatians 6:1).

See through the deception. Everything about lust is a lie. The temptress' words are "smooth" (5:3; 6:24; 7:5). She flatters her victim, appealing to his pride (7:13-15, 21). She pretends to be religious, making him feel less dirty with a "girl-next-door" respectability (7:14). She promises pleasure without consequences (7:16-20; 9:17). Yet, Proverbs repeatedly warns of the inevitable trouble sensuality brings (5:4-6, 9-14; 6:26-35; 7:21-27; 9:18). Sin's momentary sweetness quickly turns to enduring bitterness (5:3-4), and even to eternal destruction (5:5; 9:18).

Enjoy sex with your wife. For those who are married, satisfying marital intimacy is part of Scripture's strategy for mainting moral purity (5:15-19; 1 Corinthians 7:1-5).

Fear God. As sobering as the "horizontal" effects of sensuality are, Proverbs 5 climaxes its warnings against lust with the "vertical" factor in verse 21. God sees everything—even deleted browsing histories. Fearing the Lord is key to departing from evil (16:6).

Delight in Christ. The most significant way to battle lust isn't external, as important as filters and accountability may be. Lust is a heart issue, and it requires a heart solution. What the simpleton of Proverbs 5-9 needed was gospel wisdom (5:1-2; 6:20-23; 7:1-4; chs. 8-9). The gospel delivers us from sin both by breaking its hold (Romans 6) and exceeding its joy. Notice in chapter 9 how Lady Wisdom uses the same pleasure language as the adulteress (9:1-6, 13-18). That's significant. We're not just warned away from the feast of sin; we're invited to the feast of the gospel. We don't just flee the tempter; we follow Jesus, Wisdom incarnate (Matthew 12:42; 1 Corinthians 1:24). We flee youthful passions *by* pursuing righteousness (2 Timothy 2:22). Brothers, fight sin by delighting in Christ, Who alone can satisfy.

Let the gospel provide pleasures which surpass sensuality. —CHRIS

As Christ Loved the Church
READ 1 CORINTHIANS 13

*Husbands, love your wives, as Christ loved the church
and gave himself up for her.*
EPHESIANS 5:25

First Corinthians 13, often called "The Love Chapter," is one of the most famous passages in the Bible. Paul uses the word *love* nine times in the chapter and describes it in sixteen ways. While the love he describes is not primarily intended for married couples, it most certainly applies to them. There are at least three ways in which "The Love Chapter" can be specifically applied to Christian husbands.

Christlike love matters more than anything else in your marriage (13:1-3).
Paul is talking to Christians who have amazing gifts and abilities, lots of biblical knowledge, and a long track record of helping out needy people. Yet, these Christians still lack selfless, humble love toward each other. Christian husband, it's possible for you to do lots of kind things for your wife, but never once do them out of love. You can be a good provider, a respectable parent, and a faithful husband, yet still be lacking in the one quality that really matters to God: love. Spiritual gifts, understanding, and self-sacrifice are meaningless—even obnoxious—without love.

You'll show the most Christlike love for your wife when she irritates you (13:4-7).
The love that God is calling you to display isn't fully shown until life gets messy. Notice some of Paul's less-than-romantic descriptions of love: *Love is patient (13:4). Love doesn't keep a list of wrongs suffered (13:5). Love bears all things, hopes all things, endures all things (13:7).* Do you see what's implied here? Unless someone offends you, you don't need to be *patient*. Unless someone wrongs you, you don't need to *refuse to keep a list of wrongs*. Unless someone annoys you, you don't need to *bear all things*. Unless someone disappoints you, you don't need to *hope all things*. Unless someone hurts you, you don't need to *endure all things*. In other words, the love that God calls you to show your wife assumes that she is going to offend you, wrong you, annoy you, disappoint you, and hurt you. And when she does, you have a prime opportunity to show her and others what Jesus' love is really like, because Christlike love is magnified when it's poured out on sinners. As Kent Hughes told the men in his church, "[M]arriage will reveal something about [your wife] which you already know about yourself—that she is a sinner. Marriage reveals everything: her weaknesses, her worst inconsistencies, the things others never see. *Loving your spouse is not to love her as a saint, but as a sinner*" (*Disciplines of a Godly Man*, p. 37, italics original).

God calls you to be the leader in Christlike love. In Ephesians 5:25 Paul, the same author who wrote 1 Corinthians 13, commands Christian husbands to be the leaders in showing this love in their marriage: "Husbands, love your wives, as Christ loved the church and gave himself up for her." Jesus Christ Himself is the example you're called to imitate. He sacrificed Himself for His bride, the church. He constantly seeks the church's growth. He personally cares for the church's needs and cherishes her in her struggles. Like Christ, you should be the leader in love. Don't wait for your wife to initiate love or deserve it. Be the one to pursue peace after an argument, the one to initiate reconciliation after harsh words. Why? Because you're the leader. Because God calls you to love your wife like Christ loves the church.

Let the gospel shape your love for your wife. —JOE

Values, Vices, & Virtues

READ COLOSSIANS 3

Whatever you do, in word or deed,
do everything in the name of the Lord Jesus.
COLOSSIANS 3:17

The book of Colossians contains some of the most glorious expressions of Christian doctrine in all of Scripture. For the first two chapters, Paul fights false teaching by presenting Christ as the only Son, Creator, and Savior. He insists that there is salvation only in Jesus, and thus there must be no turning from Him or adding to Him. Christ is more than enough. The book doesn't end at chapter two, however. In typical fashion, Paul applies the rich truths of the book to everyday life. Justification (being *declared* righteous *in* Christ) results in ongoing sanctification (being *made* righteous *like* Christ) until in heaven we reach glorification (being *entirely* righteous *with* Christ). Colossians 3 shows us how to progress in our sanctification.

First, keep loving what is above (3:1-4). Paul begins by addressing the heart—our affections. Christianity flows from the inside out. Affections determine actions; belief determines behavior. Thus, Paul reminds believers that they've been united to Christ's death (2:20; 3:3) and resurrection (3:1; Romans 6) and will be united with Him at His return (3:4). In light of this union, he urges them to treasure the things of Christ rather than the things of the world—not in a theoretical way, but in a life-changing way.

Second, keep fighting your sins (3:5-9, 11). Our union with Christ's death and resurrection may give the impression that the battle is over; nothing could be further from the truth. There is an ongoing struggle, and there is no easy solution. Reading a book won't end temptation, nor will responding to a sermon, praying a prayer, or binding a demon (the main problem is "in you," not outside of you; 3:5; Matthew 5:18-20). Whereas we have put off the old self (3:9), we're still commanded to battle residual sins. Two pictures are drawn to describe our efforts against our flesh: we are to put our sins to death like a deadly enemy (3:5), and we are to put away our sins like a filthy garment (3:8). Paul specifically condemns sexual sins (3:5), interpersonal sins (like anger, harsh words, and deception; 3:8-9), and prejudice (3:11). He reminds us that these are the very things that are bringing God's wrath on the world (3:6; and implicitly, which brought God's wrath on Christ). He tells us that these sins typified our old way of life; we don't live like that anymore (1 Corinthians 6:9-11).

Finally, keep reflecting your Savior (3:10, 12-17). It's tempting to measure spirituality merely on the basis of prohibitions—what we don't do. But we are called to Christlikeness (3:10), which is active, not passive—the adoption of virtues, not just the avoidance of vices. This is a vital truth to understand: whereas the image of God in mankind (Genesis 1:26) was morally marred by the Fall, it's being redeemed by the gospel. Our "new self" is "being renewed in knowledge after the image of its creator" (3:10). So the Christian who is growing will increasingly be like Christ (Romans 8:28-29; 2 Corinthians 3:18). He will cultivate Christian virtues (3:12-17). He will be compassionate, kind, humble, meek, and patient (3:12). He will forbear and forgive (3:13). He will be loving, peaceful, and thankful (3:14-15). He will delight in the gospel and share it in word and song (3:16). And he will give God glory for all of it (3:17).

The Christian life described in Colossians 3 is rather mundane. God's not calling us to perform miracles or receive visions. He's calling us to spend the rest of our lives cultivating eternal values, fighting deep-rooted vices, and growing in Christlike virtues.

Let the gospel change you from the inside out. —CHRIS

Your One & Only Command
READ EPHESIANS 1–2

Fathers, do not provoke your children to anger,
but bring them up in the discipline and instruction of the Lord.
EPHESIANS 6:4

Ephesians 6:4 is the only place in the New Testament where fathers are given a positive command by God. It's the only place where we're told what to do, in additic to what *not* to do. Isn't that amazing? God gave fathers one sentence! We have one basic command: "Bring your children up in the instruction and counsel of the Lord Jesus." We'll briefly unpack the significance of this command, but before doing that, we need to consider the four prerequisites to carrying it out successfully.

Prerequisite 1: You must never get over God's grace to you. In order to fulfill your responsibility as a *father*, you must stand in awe of what God has done for you as a *sinner*. God's command to you as a father is rooted in the amazing grace He's shown you (Ephesians 1-3). Never forget that you used to be dead in your sins and that Go miraculously raised you to life. You have a calling to walk worthy of (4:1).

Prerequisite 2: Don't think you have what it takes. Notice that Ephesians 6:4 is rooted in the command, "Do not get drunk with wine…but be filled with the Spirit" (5:18). Dad, you cannot rightly raise your children unless you are continually controlled by God's indwelling Holy Spirit.

Prerequisite 3: Be the most humble servant in your family. When a Christian man is Spirit-filled (5:18), it's evident in his servant-mindedness (5:21). That has everything to do with parenting. Dad, you must exercise your ministry with Christli humility. You're the leader of your home. But that doesn't mean that you get to be th boss, the one everybody else serves! It means that you get to be the biggest servant.

Prerequisite 4: Be afraid of your potential for destroying your children. "Do not provoke your children to anger" (6:4a; Colossians 3:21). We can provoke our childre in so many ways: harshness, inconsistency, condescension, favoritism, neglect, or hypocrisy. Although children bear responsibility for their own choices, a father who provokes them bears much greater guilt.

Your only command: Bring them up in Christ's instruction. Once you've earned credibility by your genuine love for Christ and consistent growth in Christlikeness, you have to actually *teach your children about Him*. Example leads to instruction. Notice a few details about this command. First, it's not directed to *mothers* or *parents* but specifically to *fathers*. This is your responsibility. Second, "bring them up" implie that your instruction begins when your child is very young (in a highchair) and ends when your child is a follower of Jesus (independent of you). In other words, your goa in "bringing them up" is not conformity, but maturity. Third, "in the discipline and instruction of the Lord" implies that you have a Christ-centered message and that you verbally communicate it. When does this instruction happen? It should happen in times that are more formal, like bedtime stories and family devotions, but also in times that are informal: "when you sit in your house, and when you walk by the way, and when you lie down, and when you rise" (Deuteronomy 6:7). This is 24-7 instruction about the Lord Jesus Christ from a grace-saturated, Spirit-controlled, servant-minded father.

Let the gospel help you point your children to Christ. —JOE

A Romance Primer for Husbands

READ SONG OF SONGS 4:1–5:1

You have captivated my heart with one glance of your eyes.
SONG OF SONGS 4:9

o many men, the concept of marital romance is as girly as a chick-flick. They think
nat being romantic is only for men with a certain personality or for those who don't
wear the pants in the family." However, because a husband's relationship with his wife
nould picture Jesus' own *cherishing* of the church, romance is not an option for Christian
usbands. Jesus' love for His church is not cold commitment. It's not a harsh "I told you
0 years ago that I loved you; I'll let you know if that ever changes." God calls you to
omance your wife. The Bible's most explicit example of a romantic husband is found in
ne Song of Songs. Here are ten inspired lessons from the Song for romancing your bride.

irst, talk intimately with your wife. Husbands are often known for their lack of
ommunication, especially *romantic* communication. Solomon, however, speaks almost
0% of the words in this romantic book. He also takes the initiative in arranging this
whole collection of romantic poems. Face-to-face conversations, romantic middle-of-
ne-day phone calls, playful emails, and "just because" love notes can intoxicate your
rife's heart. *Second,* complement your wife's beauty. Solomon calls his wife "the most
eautiful among women" (1:8; see 1:15; 2:2, 10, 13; 4:1, 7; 6:4, 10; 7:6). He lets her
now that he loves everything about her—her hair, cheeks, neck, eyes, nose, teeth, lips,
ongue, mouth, breasts, belly, thighs, and feet (see 4:1-11; 7:1-5). He's enthralled with
er beauty, and he lets her know it in great detail. *Third,* constantly assure your wife of
our exclusive devotion. Solomon's wife knows that his affections are completely for her
2:4, 16; 6:3; 7:10), that he loves to be with her (2:8, 14), and that his heart is totally
aptivated by her (1:9-10; 2:2; 4:9). Men, you must communicate this to your wife by
oth your words and actions. *Fourth,* remember that your fragrance matters to your
rife. Yes, the Bible talks about personal hygiene. Who knew! You can show great love to
our wife by paying attention to the smell of your body and breath (1:3; 5:16). *Fifth,*
ake the lead in evaluating and protecting your relationship. Solomon's wife asks him to
vatch out for "little foxes" that can destroy their garden of pleasure (2:15). You should
ake the initiative in identifying and dealing with threats to your marriage, seeking your
rife's advice on how to strengthen your relationship. *Sixth,* show love in planning special
ccasions. Solomon takes the time to find a location for private lovemaking (1:16-17), to
lan a springtime getaway (2:8-14), and to organize an elaborate entourage for his bride
n their wedding day (3:6-11). Follow his example. *Seventh,* spend time in lovemaking.
Jnselfish sex isn't just "Get your pleasure and be done." Slow down. Seriously! "Enjoy
he garden. Drink the wine. Eat the fruit. Climb the tree. Graze in the field. Smell the
lowers" (4:16-5:1; 6:2; 7:9, 13; 8:2). *Eighth,* cultivate an appreciation of nature and
oetry. While men are often ambivalent toward these things, it's clear from this book
hat using poetic language with imagery from nature can show romantic love for your
rife. If your wife enjoys culture or wildlife, you'd better learn to, as well. *Ninth,* refer
o your wife with terms of endearment. Notice that Solomon has at least eight different
ersonal expressions by which he calls his wife: "my love" (1:9; 2:2, 10, 13; 4:1, 7; 5:2),
my beautiful one" (2:10, 13), "my dove" (2:14; 5:2; 6:9), "my bride" (4:8-12; 5:1), "my
ister" (4:9-10, 12; 5:1-2), "my perfect one" (5:2; 6:9), "noble daughter" (7:1), and "loved
ne" (7:6). *Finally,* touch your wife often. Solomon's bride delights in how he touches
er, both sexually and non-sexually. She loves how he kisses her (1:2; 5:13, 16), snuggles
vith her (1:13; 2:17), touches her (5:4), and embraces her (2:6; 8:3).

et the gospel be the reason you show more romantic love for your wife. —JOE

Why We Need Fellowship
READ ECCLESIASTES 4

Two are better than one....Woe to him who is alone.
ECCLESIASTES 4:9-10

Guys like their space. One of the most evident differences between men and women i
our approach to friendships. Men don't want to be invited to a "Meeting of the Mind
in the Men's Room," thanks. And having a buddy write us a note that ends with "You
BFF" will probably end the friendship, not advance it. Guys are usually loners. But
even if we acknowledge that male friendships will look different than those of their
female counterparts, we still need Christian friends. *Need*, I say. Ecclesiastes 4:7-12
describes the benefits of a true friend (study it out) and gives a grave warning about
isolating ourselves: "Woe to him who is alone" (4:10). Proverbs similarly extols the
value of godly friendships (Proverbs 17:17; 27:17). It's not until the New Testament,
however, that we get a full-orbed understanding of Christian fellowship.

True fellowship requires personal engagement. The word *fellowship* sounds easy
enough. It brings to mind images of potlucks, softball games, maybe even a game
night (though that's probably pushing it for many guys). However, the biblical term
for fellowship is a lot more meaningful. It describes engagement—having things in
"common" (the basic meaning of the Greek word *koinonia*). When we were joined to
Christ (Ephesians 2:1-13), we were simultaneously joined to Christians (Ephesians
2:14-22). Fellowship displays that union. It includes partnership in gospel advance
(Philippians 1:5), deep Christian unity (Philippians 2:1), and even financial assistance
when necessary (Romans 15:26). Fellowship was one of the four main practices of the
early church (Acts 2:42). You can't read through the epistles without being struck by
the social dimension of Christianity.

True fellowship requires gospel instruction. Men are professionals at talking about
everything in order to talk about nothing. Listen to the average conversation among
men at church. We talk about weather, fishing, hunting, cars, sports, and business.
In short, we talk to fellow Christians about the same nonsense we talk to strangers
about. It shouldn't be that way. Imagine having Christian friends who talk about the
sermon after the service. Imagine conversations which focus on the word of Christ
(Colossians 3:16). That's the way it's supposed to be. We should be contributing to ea
other's spiritual growth as a Christian community (Ephesians 4:11-16). We should be
encouraging one another, loving one another, comforting one another, and obeying th
rest of the ubiquitous "one another" commands of the New Testament.

True fellowship requires humble transparency. Fellowship demands that we get real.
Too many men show up for church each Sunday with their "game faces" on. We tell
each other that we're doing "Great, praise God!" But we're not. We're discouraged.
We're fighting with our wives. We're battling our teens. We're losing the war with
pornography. We don't need church friends to *think* we're okay; we need them to
help us *get there*! We're supposed to rescue our brothers who are suffocating beneath a
besetting sin (Galatians 6:1; James 5:19-20), but in order to do so we need to foster a
culture of transparency in which we can admit that we're struggling, ask for prayer, an
accept instruction. In other words, *fellowship*.

One of the most essential things a Christian can do is to be active in a Bible-teaching
church. Find one. Join it. Get to its services. And by all means, encourage fellowship
among its men through meaningful, transparent, gospel-centered friendships.

Let the gospel produce relationships with godly friends. —CHRIS

The Chain Reaction of Reconciliation

READ 2 CORINTHIANS 5

We implore you on behalf of Christ, be reconciled to God.
2 CORINTHIANS 5:20

As a boy, I loved unleashing domino "chain reactions" on my kitchen floor. I loved seeing how energy was received by one piece of plastic, passed on to the next, and so on. Even better was watching the epic domino chains on television. As an adult, I get far greater delight out of *spiritual* chain reactions in Christ's church. The New Testament constantly describes Christians receiving blessings, then passing them on. We receive love, then extend it (1 John 4:19). We receive comfort, then extend it (2 Corinthians 1:3-4). We receive forgiveness, then extend it (Ephesians 4:32). And we receive reconciliation, then extend it. Reconciliation is one of the most vivid of the biblical depictions of salvation. It's described with particular clarity in 2 Corinthians 5:17-6:1, where it's mentioned five times.

We needed reconciliation. 2 Corinthians 5:17 is a beloved verse about the new life we have in Christ. Part of the old life that "has passed away" is our enmity with God (5:18-19). The concept of reconciliation assumes that God and sinners are at war. The hostility between God and sinners moves in both directions. We are hostile toward Him. Ever since the Garden of Eden, we've been rebelling against Him and running from Him. We're aliens, exiles, enemies (Ephesians 2:12). And we don't even desire reconciliation. Worse for us, God is hostile toward us. He can't tolerate our sin. He's against us. We have an omnipotent Enemy, which means we're damned. Amazingly, God *does* desire reconciliation, in spite of us.

God granted us reconciliation through Christ. 2 Corinthians 5:18 says that God has initiated reconciliation. In fact, He's entirely accomplished it: "All this is from God." He has made peace with sinners, and He's done so "through Christ" and "in Christ" (5:18-19), by judging Him for sin in our place (5:21; Romans 5:6-11; Ephesians 2:14-18). My friend and mentor Michael Barrett describes it this way: "It is by the gospel of Jesus Christ that the Lord has graciously, yet justly, removed the impediments to peace and fellowship between Himself and sinners" (*Complete in Him*, p. 148). By reconciling us, God brought both "peace" (the end of enmity) and "fellowship" (the beginning of communion). That's huge. Reconciliation is God's pursuit of a relationship with us. We don't just get peace, or forgiveness, or heaven. We get God!

God entrusted us with reconciliation. Our personal peace with God is only part of what God is doing in the world. 2 Corinthians 5:18-20 teaches that God begins a "reconciliation chain reaction" each time He grants salvation. The moment we are reconciled we become partners in the great work of reconciliation. God has entrusted to us both the "ministry of reconciliation" (5:18) and "the message of reconciliation" (5:19). If that weren't staggering enough, we're called "ambassadors for Christ" (5:20). He makes His gospel appeal (or *plea*, NKJV) through us (5:20). We speak to sinners on His behalf, urging them to "be reconciled to God."

I rejoice that God has reconciled me to Himself through His Son. But I can't imagine a more sacred trust. I'm responsible to tell sinners that they're estranged from God. I've been commanded to urge them to be reconciled to Him by faith in Christ. So have you. We dare not alter that message, and we dare not neglect that ministry. For those who have been freely reconciled to God, life is one giant ministry of reconciliation. *Life is mission*—whether at the office or on the other side of the world.

Let the gospel give your life a missionary purpose. —CHRIS

When God Tells a Man to "Man Up"

READ JOB 38:1–40:14

Dress for action like a man;
I will question you, and you make it known to me.

JOB 40:7

Men who suffer—even godly men—know what it's like to deal with bitterness toward God. Job really suffered, and Job really struggled with God's fairness. Although Job responded in an exemplary way to his suffering, he didn't respond perfectly. He was a great man, but he was just a man. Throughout his affliction there were a few occasions when Job let God have it: "Leave me alone" (7:11-21); "Stop condemning me when I'm innocent" (10:1-7); "I want to take You to court, and I know I'm right" (ch. 13); "You're not being fair" (ch. 24); "I don't deserve this" (ch. 31). Job never did what Satan said he would do (1:11), yet Job did charge God (as Derek Kidner puts it) with "bullying" and "calculated cruelty" (*The Wisdom of Proverbs, Job and Ecclesiastes*, pp. 64-65).

What kind of counsel did Job need in his time of suffering? Not the kind his "friends" gave him! Job needed wisdom that no human counselor could give. The Lord came to him in a terrifying way—"out of the whirlwind" (38:1). He told Job, "Brace yourself like a man" (38:3, NIV). In response to Job's audacious challenges, God began to ask him questions that were too difficult for him to answer: "Where were you when I created the earth" (38:4-7)? "Have you been making the sun come up every day" (38:12-15)? "Can you control violent weather" (38:22-24)? "Did you design the hawks and eagles to fly like they fly, live where they live, and hunt like they hunt" (39:26-30)? By the end of chapter 39, God had asked Job about eighty questions, concluding with, "Do you really want to 'contend with the Almighty'" (40:1)? Job immediately repented and shut his mouth, worn out by God's barrage. But the Lord wasn't finished with him. He confronted Job with dozens of more questions about terrifying creatures (chs. 40-41).

Job wisely surrendered, saying that the view of God's power and his weakness is exactly what he needed (42:1-6). Job needed a fresh encounter with his sovereign God (42:5), as does every suffering saint. It's instructive that God pulled "the sovereignty card" rather than "the love card" in answering Job. In God's climactic speech (chs. 38-41) He didn't ask Job, "Don't you see how *good* I am? Don't you remember how I gave you wealth and success and children? Don't you know that your suffering's not as bad as it could have been?" All of those things were true. The Lord was certainly "compassionate and merciful" (James 5:11). But Job's primary need at this time was not a tender assurance of God's love. Job needed a humbling reminder of God's sovereignty. He needed to fear the Lord more deeply—to remember that the two of them weren't peers.

When we're freshly reminded of God's glory and greatness, we're reminded that He's worth serving just for who He is. The book of Job was written, as Joseph Caryl wrote in the 17th century, to combat the idea "that the people of God serve him for their own ends…and to show that His people *follow him for love*; for the excellency they find in him, and in his service. Though he strip them naked of all they have, yet they will cleave to him" (*An Exposition of Job*, p. xii, italics original). Is serving Jesus worth all the suffering? That depends on how great you think He is. If Jesus Christ really is the image of the invisible God, the radiance of God's glory, the One by Whom and for Whom all things were created, and the One Who upholds the universe by His powerful word, then simply knowing Him is enough to satisfy us when we suffer the loss of all things (Colossians 1:16-18; Hebrews 1:3; Philippians 3:8-10).

Let the gospel satisfy you in your suffering. —JOE

Gentle Leadership
READ MARK 10:42-45 & JOHN 13:1-17

Husbands, love your wives, and do not be harsh with them.
COLOSSIANS 3:19

Despite modern protestations to the contrary, Scripture repeatedly addresses men as the heads of their homes (1 Corinthians 11:3; Ephesians 5:23). The man's responsibility to lead in the home and church rests not on cultural norms of the day, but on God's design from creation (1 Corinthians 11:8-9; 1 Timothy 2:8-15). The Bible teaches authority in the home, church, and society and requires submission to it.

That's not all that Scripture says about leadership, however. Christian men are often more prepared to cite verses that establish them as leaders than verses that *limit* and *define* that leadership. In light of the heavy-handed authority that was accepted in the Roman world during the New Testament era (when wives, children, and servants were treated as property), it's fascinating to me that the Bible repeatedly forbids leaders to abuse their God-given authority. Almost every time the New Testament epistles command submission to authority, they immediately command those exercising that authority to do so *with grace*.

Husbands should lead their wives gently. When Scripture commands wives to submit to their husbands (Ephesians 5:22-24; Colossians 3:18; 1 Peter 3:1-6), it immediately commands husbands to lead their wives in a loving, self-sacrificing manner:

> *"Husbands, love your wives, as Christ loved the church and gave himself up for her.... Husbands should love their wives as their own bodies....[Nourish and cherish her].... Let each of you love his wife as himself" (Ephesians 5:25, 28, 29, 33).*

> *"Husbands, love your wives, and do not be harsh with them" (Colossians 3:19).*

> *"Husbands, live with your wives in an understanding way, showing honor to the woman as the weaker vessel" (1 Peter 3:7).*

Fathers should lead their children gently. After requiring children to obey their parents (Ephesians 6:1-3; Colossians 3:20), Scripture warns parents (and fathers in particular) against exasperating their children. Unnecessary rigidity, verbal and physical harshness, lack of affection, favoritism, hypocrisy, and pettiness devastate a family and drive children toward the world. You can either lord your authority over your children or influence them for Christ. You can't do both.

> *"Fathers, do not provoke your children to anger, but bring them up in the discipline and instruction of the Lord" (Ephesians 6:4).*

> *"Fathers, do not provoke your children, lest they become discouraged" (Colossians 3:21).*

Scripture similarly prescribes humble leadership in the workplace (Ephesians 6:9; Colossians 4:1) and church (1 Peter 5:1-4; 1 Timothy 3:3; 2 Timothy 2:24-26)—topics worth additional study. What's clear is that the Bible leaves no room for the arrogant huffing and puffing that some men display in the home and church under the guise of Christian leadership. There's nothing Christian about it. Christ taught and modeled selfless leadership (John 13:1-17; Mark 10:42-45). Yes, men, we're leaders. But are we Christlike leaders?

Let the gospel transform you into a gentle leader. —CHRIS

The Anchor for Your Soul

READ HEBREWS 6–7

We have this as a sure and steadfast anchor of the soul,
a hope that enters into the inner place behind the curtain.
HEBREWS 6:19

In view of our weaknesses, our regular failures, and the unknown future, how can we certain that we'll persevere in faith to the end? Asked in another way, in view of the s of our little boat and the threatening weather forecast, how can we be certain that we never capsize? The writer to the Hebrews tells us that our boat will never overturn— that we'll endure in faith and "inherit the promises" (6:12)—because we have "an anchor of the soul" (6:19).

What exactly is this anchor? The answer may surprise you. The anchor that keeps us afloat is the truth about Jesus in Psalm 110:4: "The Lord has sworn and will not char his mind, 'You are a priest forever after the order of Melchizedek.'" (Notice that Psalm 110:4 is the writer's clear focus in Hebrews 6:17, 20.) Have you ever been encourage that your Priest is ordained *by an oath of God*? Have you ever been deeply comforted know that you have a Priest *after the order of Melchizedek*? Sadly, I don't think that m believers have experienced the specific comfort of Psalm 110:4. "What does an oath have to do with my trials? Melchizedek who?" Let me describe for you your anchor.

You have an unshakable anchor. The first words of Psalm 110:4 are, "The Lord has sworn and will not change His mind." Notice that God is making an oath here. Does that seem odd to you? When God wants us to know that He'll keep His promises, He doesn't *have to* swear an oath. His word stands, period. His *yes* is *yes*, and His *no* i *no*. When He made His covenant with Abraham, He didn't swear an oath (6:13-15). So why did He do so here? Because He's speaking to us on our level. When we want to confirm the certainty of our words, we take an oath (6:16). So even though God's never-changing character is enough to ensure the certainty of His promise, He swore oath so that we'd be doubly certain. Doubly certain of what? That Christ is our High Priest. God swore an oath so that "we who have fled [to Jesus] for refuge might have strong encouragement" as we endure the storms of life (6:18).

You have an eternal anchor. God the Father swore an oath to God the Son: "You are a priest forever after the order of Melchizedek." To be a priest "after the order of Melchizedek" means that He is "a priest forever." Christ is not a high priest "after the order of Levi" (like most other priests in the Old Testament)—priests who served for few decades and then died. Christ is our *eternal* Mediator. Jesus is our God-appointed High Priest Who is representing us right now in the throne room of God. And He will *never* stop interceding for us (6:19-20). So we can most confidently sing the lyric penned by Charitie Bancroft:

> *Behold Him there! The risen Lamb, my perfect, spotless righteousness,*
> *The Great unchangeable I Am, the King of Glory and of Grace,*
> *One with Himself I cannot die; my soul is purchased by His blood;*
> *My life is hid with Christ on high—with Christ my Savior and my God.*

"My life is hid with Christ on high" is the rock-solid assurance that will anchor your soul throughout every storm in life. Though the howling winds and raging waves threaten to capsize your boat, they never will. You're anchored in Jesus.

Let the gospel be your anchor through life's trials. —JOE

Exercise That Lasts
READ 1 TIMOTHY 4

*Train yourself for godliness; for while bodily training is of some value,
godliness is of value in every way.*
1 TIMOTHY 4:7-8

It's not uncommon for the New Testament writers to appeal to the world of sports for vivid illustrations of spiritual truth (1 Corinthians 9:26; Hebrews 12:1-2; 2 Timothy 4:7). Thus, it's not surprising that Paul draws a parallel between physical exercise and spiritual exercise in 1 Timothy 4:7-8. Paul explains that Christian growth is the result of deliberate and disciplined effort, and he urges us to pump some spiritual iron.

Godliness requires consistent training. The goal of every Christian should be to grow in godliness, a goal which Paul keeps before us by mentioning *godliness* nine times in the book of 1 Timothy. From the moment we are born again (an immediate, one-time event), we begin to progress in our sanctification (an ongoing process). God uses means like the Scriptures, prayer, the church, and even trials to change our character from its natural, selfish condition to the image of Jesus Christ (Romans 8:29; 2 Corinthians 3:18; Colossians 3:10). The same gospel that saves us from sin also changes us. We'll not be sinless until we're with Christ in heaven, but we'll certainly be *sinning less* as we grow in godliness. What is especially vital for us to understand is this: *Godliness is the result of effort*—focused effort that turns us away from useless distractions (1 Tim 4:7a) and consistent effort that follows an ongoing regimen of spiritual exercises. Don't lose steam after a few early morning "workouts."

Godliness requires personal responsibility. 1 Timothy 4:7 is one of many verses in which Paul tells Timothy to take care of "himself" (e.g., 1 Timothy 4:13, 15, 16). Paul couldn't make Timothy godly. His exemplary grandmother and mother couldn't make him godly. Timothy had to take responsibility for his own spiritual progress. In his classic book *The Practice of Godliness*, Jerry Bridges explains: "You and I are responsible to train ourselves. We are dependent upon God for his divine enablement, but we are responsible; we are not passive in this process" (p. 55). Acknowledge your responsibility here. Godliness isn't something some people are just born with, or simply "catch" like a spiritual cold. Godliness isn't an accident; it happens on purpose. Paul commands Timothy to do something—to train himself to be godly.

Godliness is profitable for time and eternity. Paul concludes his sports analogy in verse 8 by comparing the eternal rewards of spiritual training with the fleeting benefits of physical training. It's true that bodily exercise is valuable—a lesson which many of us would do well to consider! Watch your weight. Swim, bike, walk, or run to keep your body in shape. Knock yourself out. But your spiritual health is of far greater importance. Though your outer man is wasting away (despite your best efforts), your inner man can be renewed daily (2 Corinthians 4:16). Just as God commands ladies to beautify their hearts, not just their wardrobes and faces (1 Peter 3:3-4), He commands men to focus on their maturity, not just their muscles (1 Timothy 4:7-8).

So, what are you doing to grow toward Christlikeness? Are you resisting sin? Are you getting daily nourishment from the Scriptures? Are you enjoying God's presence through consistent prayer? Are you filling your mind with music that reminds you of the gospel throughout the day? Are you an active, teachable member of a good church? Are you making deliberate, grace-enabled efforts to advance in your walk with Christ?

Let the gospel motivate and enable you to grow in godliness. —CHRIS

Your Marital Status Is Just a Phase

READ 1 CORINTHIANS 7

As the bridegroom rejoices over the bride,
so shall your God rejoice over you.
ISAIAH 62:5

God established marriage, a one-flesh union between a man and a woman, in order to provide a sublime picture of the greater reality of the faithful love and unbreakable union that exists between Jesus Christ and His church. This means that the *gospel* is ultimate, not marriage! Christian, whether married or single, you must continually remind yourself of the Bible's teaching regarding the brevity of your marital status.

Married man, you won't be married to your wife forever. Jesus teaches in Luke 20:34-36 that there will be no marriage in heaven: "The sons of this age marry and are given in marriage, but those who are considered worthy to attain to that age and to the resurrection from the dead neither marry nor are given in marriage, for they cannot die anymore, because they are equal to angels and are sons of God, being sons of the resurrection." When Jesus says that we'll not marry because we'll be "sons of God" and "sons of the resurrection," I think He means that our relationship to God as His children will take on a dimension so deep and significant that marriage will be rendered obsolete. Leon Morris comments on this: "The absence of marriage does not mean…a leveling down of relations so that life is on a lower level. Rather it is a being taken up into the fullness of life in the family of God" (*Luke*, p. 319). If the thought of not being married to your wife forever makes you happy, I'm sorry that your marriage is less than fulfilling. But I also urge you to remember that your marriage is *intended* to be less than perfectly fulfilling. On the other hand, if it makes you sad to think that you'll not be married to your wife in heaven, I empathize. But we must also recognize that the same God who created marriage in the first place can create something that will be better—not worse—than what we presently know. We'll be more than satisfied with Him!

Single man, you won't be single forever. Singleness will not be your status is heaven. I think one of the reasons there will be no marriages in heaven is because the status of every person in heaven (in a "census" sense) will be *married*. As Alec Motyer writes about Isaiah 62:4-5, "The Lord will enjoy honeymoon-delight with those whom the Anointed One has saved and made right with him" (*The Prophecy of Isaiah*, p. 506). Revelation 19:6-7 and 21:1-9 also indicate that eternity with Christ will be something comparable to (but far exceeding) the relational depth of marriage. And in one sense, that status is true of you right now. Even if you're single, you're "married." Ephesians 5:22-33 teaches that if you are part of Christ's church, you are part of His bride. And you are experiencing just the tip of the iceberg of the wonderful reality to which every marriage is pointing (see also Romans 7:4-6).

So will we be married in heaven? In one sense, *no*. And in another sense, *yes*. Will we be single in heaven? In one sense, *no*. And in another sense, *yes*. Your marriage is not supreme. Your singleness won't last forever. So glorify God in your marriage and in your singleness by treating neither as ultimate (1 Corinthians 7:29-31). Marriage points to the gospel. Value the gospel as ultimate, and hold your current marital status lightly. It could change in a minute, and it *will* change in eternity.

Let the gospel teach to appreciate your marital status in light of eternity. —JOE

A Biblical Theology of Work
READ PROVERBS 6 & EPHESIANS 6

Aspire to live quietly...and to work with your hands.
1 THESSALONIANS 4:11

Work is a four-letter word in our "TGIF" culture. It's something even Christians yearn to get past, by getting either to the weekend (short-term) or to retirement (long-term). Yet, the Bible speaks highly of sweat-inducing, mind-taxing work. Here's a summary.

God works. Genesis 1 records God's creative labors. Genesis 2:2 explicitly says that God "rested from all his work that he had done." Jesus defends His work on the Sabbath by saying that His Father works (John 5:17). Work isn't demeaning. It's God-like.

We work as bearers of God's image. Genesis 1:26-28 records God's mandate of human "dominion" over the rest of creation at the same time it records humanity's creation in God's image. God gave humanity a job to do—before the Fall (Genesis 2:15)! Work is an evidence of our being made in the image of God, not a result of sin (though the Fall did make it more difficult; Genesis 3:17-19).

God regulated Israel's work. God repeatedly addressed His people's work habits through the Mosaic Law (Exodus 20:8-11; Leviticus 23:22; and Deuteronomy 25:4). God esteems work to be important enough to warrant His instructions. It matters.

Proverbs commends work and condemns laziness. Proverbs 6:6-11, for example, uses the ant as an example of industriousness. Diligence demonstrates wisdom, and laziness demonstrates our innate sinfulness.

Christ worked hard during His earthly ministry. Jesus was known in His day as a carpenter (Mark 6:3). Even as a healer and teacher, He worked long days (Matthew 15:30-32). Further, His teaching contained frequent allusions to farming, shepherding, and investing.

Biblical heroes worked hard in various careers. The most esteemed men from sacred history are men who had calluses on their hands. Moses and David worked as shepherds. Peter and John worked as fishermen. Paul worked as a tentmaker and highlighted his work ethic as a significant portion of his Christian testimony and gospel-advancing ministry (1 Thessalonians 2:9; Acts 20:33-35).

Christians must work conscientiously. The Bible uses a lot of ink telling employees to be industrious (Colossians 3:22-25; 1 Peter 2:18), employers to be fair (Colossians 4:1), and providers (especially men) to be faithful (1 Thessalonians 4:11-12; 1 Timothy 5:8). In fact, unrepentant laziness warrants church discipline (2 Thessalonians 3:6-14)!

Christians must work in order to give. Although our motivations for our careers can easily become selfish and worldly, the Bible commands working in part so that we can help others who cannot work (Acts 2:44-45; 4:32-37; 20:35; Ephesians 4:28) and give generously to gospel endeavors (3 John 5-8).

Work opens doors for evangelism. Paul urged professing Christians to demonstrate a sound work ethic to enhance the reputation of the gospel (1 Timothy 6:1-2). Hard work is an evidence of the gospel and a vital part of the Christian's testimony.

Work is a noble thing, especially for the redeemed. Don't endure it. Enjoy it for the glory of God (Ecclesiastes 2:24-25; 3:12-13).

Let the gospel inform and inspire your work. —CHRIS

Gospel-Rooted Peace of Mind

READ PHILIPPIANS 4

And the peace of God, which surpasses all understanding,
will guard your hearts and your minds in Christ Jesus.

PHILIPPIANS 4:7

What are the primary differences between you and non-Christians? It's easy to answer that question by jumping to externals. But you don't need to become a Christian to stop smoking, get a haircut, and start going to church. Anyone can turn over a new leaf. What primarily distinguishes Christians is something internal—a new nature that results in new thinking, not just new behavior. Here's where I think many Christian men have a blind spot. We're prone to conform to a set of Christian habits on the outside even as we remain unchanged inwardly. We're as worried, pessimistic, irritable, joyless, and argumentative as our unsaved neighbors. Many Christian men fail to evidence one of the clearest marks of Christianity—*the peace of God*. In Philippians 4:4-6 Paul urges Christians to three mental disciplines that will result in the peace of God.

First, rejoice always (4:4). It may surprise you to know that God commands your *constant happiness*. In fact, He commands it twice. As if you might miss the point, Paul repeats himself: "Rejoice…. Again, I will say, rejoice." This doesn't mean that you always have to sport a cheesy grin. But it does mean that you should always be joyful, regardless of your circumstances. Paul doesn't say, "Rejoice in your circumstances because it could be worse." No, he says, "Rejoice *in the Lord*." You need to root your happiness in the Lord Jesus—who He is, what He's like, and what He's done.

Second, be mild (4:5). Are you easily annoyed? Are you quickly offended? Do people have to walk on pins and needles when they're around you? Though such irritability is all too common among Christian men, it's contrary to clear biblical instructions. You're commanded in Philippians 4:5 to be *reasonable*—the exact opposite of *irritable*. Your mildness should be motivated by Jesus' imminent return: the Lord is "just around the corner." When Jesus returns, He'll right every wrong. So you can be mild, even when life is unjust.

Third, never worry (4:6). The Lord doesn't allow you to worry at all. "Be anxious for nothing" (4:6). Instead, He commands you to pray, and to do so all the time. Take all the things you could worry about and cast them on your Savior in a spirit of thankfulness.

These are three *mental disciplines*. Martyn Lloyd-Jones emphasized that "the main art of spiritual living" is mental discipline; it's talking to yourself rather than letting yourself talk to you (*Spiritual Depression*, pp. 20-21). The result of obeying Paul's three commands in Philippians 4:4-6 will be peace—peace that doesn't even make sense in the midst of trials! In fact, the peace of God will guard your hearts and minds like soldiers guard a city. (See how *guard* is used in 2 Corinthians 11:32.) In other words, if you discipline yourself to rejoice in the Lord Jesus, to respond reasonably to injustices in view of Jesus' soon return, and to take your worries to Him, you won't just have the peace of God—it will have you!

Let the gospel give you inexplicable peace in the midst of daily chaos. —JOE

Who Are the Church's Worship Leaders?

READ 1 TIMOTHY 2

*I desire then that in every place the men should pray,
lifting holy hands without anger or quarreling.*

1 TIMOTHY 2:8

In 1 Timothy 2:1-7 Paul urges the church to pray for government authorities so that the gospel would advance. In the very next verse (2:8), the Lord essentially says, "I want the men to lead in this kind of prayer." Scripture commands men to be the distinctive leaders in the prayer life of the church.

God desires that men pray everywhere. By saying "in every place," Paul is saying, "Wherever and whenever churches meet, I want the men to be the leaders in prayer." Take a moment to visualize thousands upon thousands of local churches gathering to pray for the advance of the gospel—gatherings in which godly men are taking the lead. Awesome to consider!

God desires that men pray intensely. "Pray, lifting holy hands." This posture was quite common in the Old Testament as an expression of submission and dependence. For example, "Solomon stood before the altar of the LORD in the presence of all the assembly of Israel *and spread out his hands toward heaven,* and said, 'O LORD, God of Israel, there is no God like you'" (1 Kings 8:22-23; see also Psalm 28:2; 63:4; Lamentations 3:41). I don't think that Paul is *demanding* that you raise your hands every time you pray. He is, however, describing a Godward intensity in your spirit that will often evidence itself outwardly. Just like getting on your knees can express humility, lifting your hands can evidence the beggarly intensity of your heart.

Lest we assume God cares only about our physical posture, Paul calls for "lifting *holy* hands." God wants the men who lead in prayer to lead a holy life—not perfect, but consistent. The hands you lift in prayer should not be hands still polluted with unconfessed sin (Psalm 24:3-4).

God desires that men pray in unity. God wants men to pray "without anger or quarreling." He doesn't want men in the church to be praying when they're out of sorts with each other (Matthew 5:23-25; 1 Peter 3:7). Leading God's people in prayer when you're at odds with a brother is a hypocrisy that God doesn't want in His church. This doesn't mean that you won't have disagreements with other believers; it does mean that you'll refuse to hold a grudge or harbor a bitter spirit toward them. The minute that supposedly passionate prayer comes from the mouth of a man who hates his brother, the church has stopped living out the gospel.

God desires that men lead the church in prayer. If you're going to lead the church in prayer, begin praying in your closet and around your kitchen table. Do you lift your hands in intense private prayer? If not, don't lift them in public. Do your children see you praying unhypocritically at home? If not, don't pray at church. Before you can be a leader at church, you must be an authentic leader at home. If you're not there yet, repent. Work at cultivating a healthy prayer habit for you and your family. And ask God to make you the kind of man He desires for the sake of the gospel.

Let the gospel fuel your leadership in corporate worship. —JOE

Love Christ by Loving the Church
READ JOHN 21

Do you love me?...Feed my lambs....Tend my sheep....Feed my lambs.
JOHN 21:15–17

John 21 serves almost as a postscript to John's Gospel. Christ's atoning death and resurrection have already been recorded (chs. 18-20), and the evangelistic purpose of the book has been summarized (20:30-31). Rather than ending with a typical record of the Great Commission, John records a beautiful scene on the Galilean seaside during which Jesus appears to the disciples, feeds them, and instructs them.

Christ restores a fallen disciple. The text climaxes in the pointed, yet gracious reinstatement of Peter (21:15-17). It has often been observed that just as Peter denied Christ three times, so Jesus questioned his love three times and commended him to ministry three times. There's a gentle reproof in the reminder of Peter's unfaithfulness and boasting: "Do you love me? Are you still claiming greater fidelity to me than these, your fellow disciples?" (See Mark 14:29.) Ouch. But where Christ wounds, He also heals: "Peter, I'll still use you. Feed my sheep." What grace!

Christ defines faithful ministry. Christ's commands for Peter to care for His sheep inform Christian ministry. Shepherds are to care for His sheep in two specific ways—to "feed" them (21:15, 17) and to "tend" them (21:16). The former term describes basic nourishment and highlights the importance of teaching the Word of God to the church. The latter term describes more general leadership and care: pastors should lead sheep, protect them, and restore them when they fall. Moreover, shepherds should be gentle. Christ uses a tender term for His flock in verse 15: "Feed my *little lambs.*" Peter was impulsive. He was a tough guy. But he needed to learn to nurture younger, immature Christians rather than run over them. It's a lesson he not only learned, but passed on in 1 Peter 5:1-4.

Christ highlights the importance of the local church. Three times Jesus asks if Peter loves Him. Each time Peter affirms that he does. And each time Jesus tells Peter to care for His sheep. The implication is clear: our Lord unmistakably connects our love for Himself with our love for His church. Peter had tried to show His commitment to Jesus on his own terms—in an audacious rebuke, in ambitious jousting for position with the other disciples, in boastful promises to fight for Jesus to the death, and even in hacking off a servant's ear in a show of both ill-advised aggression and poor aim. His attempts to show his love were terribly flawed, as are so many of ours. But Christ simplified things for him and for us. "Love Me? Feed mine." We demonstrate our love for Christ by loving Christians. As we sometimes sing, "I love the church because I love her Lord." On the other hand, the opposite is true as well: to oppose Christ's church is to persecute Him personally (Acts 9:4). How encouraging to see how highly Jesus esteems the church!

John 21:15-17 should be a defining text for your involvement with a local church. No church is perfect, to be sure. But a church that believes and preaches the gospel is Christ's flock, purchased by Christ's blood (Acts 20:28). So I ask you, does your commitment to your local church indicate that you love Christ? If not, I urge you to become active in your local assembly. Show that you love the Shepherd by loving His sheep. Worship with them. Learn with them. Grow with them. Give with them. Serve with them—all because you love the Lord Jesus Christ.

Let the gospel inspire your love for your local church. —CHRIS

The Gospel for Good People
READ ROMANS 2

*In passing judgment on another you condemn yourself,
because you, the judge, practice the very same things.*

ROMANS 2:1

Charles Dickens' *A Christmas Carol* opens with these stark words: "Marley was dead to begin with....Permit me to repeat emphatically, that Marley was as dead as a doornail....There is no doubt that Marley was dead. This must be distinctly understood, or nothing wonderful can come of the story I am going to relate."

Paul says essentially the same thing in the first three chapters of his letter to the church at Rome: "All people—whether you grew up as a Jew or pagan—are sinners. All people are under the wrath of God. All people are 'dead to begin with.' If you don't understand this truth, nothing in life and nothing in the Bible will make sense."

We are all sinners. This is something that non-Christians must reckon with and that Christians must never forget! After all, Paul is writing the book of Romans *to* Christians (1:7), and he's doing so (at least in part) to cultivate their unity. Christians who come from upright and respectable backgrounds are very prone to view themselves as superior to those who come from immoral or irreligious backgrounds. Paul takes us back to the gospel, teaching that Jews and Gentiles are equally deserving of God's wrath because both are equally wicked.

Paul makes this point in a masterful way. He reminds his Jewish readers of God's wrath on pagans who are given over to sexual impurity (1:24-25), homosexuality (1:26-27), and debauchery of every kind (1:28-32). This would be like telling a group of believers in our day that God's wrath is hanging over corrupt politicians, abortionists, porn stars, and evolutionists. You can just imagine the responses from the pews: "Amen! That's right! Preach it, brother!" But then, unexpectedly, Paul sets the hook: "You yourselves are not one bit better" (2:1)!

In Romans 2, Paul teaches that those who come from a religious background are under God's condemnation as much as pagans (2:1-5). Because God is a perfectly just Judge (2:6-11), only those who perfectly live out His law will be justified in His sight (2:12-16). This means that good people must see themselves through God's eyes (2:17-24). He sees every word, every action, every thought, and every motive. And His standard of judgment is not mere external conformity, but heart purity (2:25-29)! Paul says, "Circumcision doesn't matter to God if you're a law breaker. God wants a heart that's fully devoted to Him, not just a life that looks religious on the outside" (2:25-29). In our day, it would be similar to saying, "Going to church, wearing a tie, and giving a tithe don't impress God." Such things have never made a sinner more acceptable to God. What God is interested in is not external habits and supposed piety, but a heart that clings to Christ.

Do you realize that you are no better than the worst pagan? When you internalize this truth, it will be evident in two ways. First, you will love God and revel in His grace. Although you are just as deserving of God's wrath as anyone who has ever lived, God has graciously loved you in Christ. The one who's been forgiven much loves much (Luke 7:36-50). Second, you will show God's grace to others—both non-Christians and Christians—because you understand that you are no better than they are. The gospel leaves no room for arrogance.

Let the gospel humble you. —JOE

The Papa John's Principle
READ EPHESIANS 5:18–6:4

The righteous who walks in his integrity—
blessed are his children after him!
PROVERB 20:7

Books abound which claim to deliver the secret to a happy home, the twelve steps to a model marriage, or God's path to perfect kids. Some amount to behaviorism. Man fail to urge utter dependence on God, who alone is sovereign. And few, it seems, foc on the character of the individual members of the family. Proverbs 20:7 deserves our attention. It teaches what I call "The Papa John's Principle." You remember the pizza maker's common-sense slogan: *"Better ingredients, better pizza."* Well, Proverbs 20:7 teaches that a godly home begins with godly individuals—and specifically, a godly m

A godly home begins with a man who is righteous. What does this proverb mean when it describes a man as "righteous"? It doesn't mean that he's a good guy who behaves himself. Rather, when the Old Testament speaks of the "righteous man," it's describing his standing before God on the basis of *imputed* righteousness (Genesis 15:6). The righteous man is saved by faith in Christ, to use New Testament terminology. Don't miss the significance of this: the gospel is the cornerstone of a go home. Your relationship with your family depends on your relationship with Christ.

That's why New Testament passages like Ephesians 5:22-6:4 (which address relationships in the home) come *after* passages like Ephesians 1-3 (which address the riches of salvation through Christ). You can't be a godly husband or father until you first a godly man. And you can't be a godly man apart from the gospel.

A godly home begins with a man of integrity. The same gospel that allows a sinner be declared righteous (justification) also affects his daily life (sanctification). The mar commended in Proverbs 20:7 "walks in his integrity." The Hebrew word translated a *integrity* means "completeness." It describes a man whose character isn't deficient or inconsistent. He's not perfect, but he's humbly progressing. His religion doesn't look good at church and bad at the office. His *walk*—his everyday life, in private and in public—is characterized by godliness.

Once again this concept is advanced in the book of Ephesians. Though Ephesians focuses on our position in Christ (as described above), it repeatedly (six times in six chapters!) instructs Christians to "walk" in a manner consistent with their faith—to walk with integrity (2:10; 4:1, 17; 5:2, 8, 15). It's no accident that Paul's relational commands occur later in the book. Paul speaks to husbands and wives (5:22-33), to children and parents (6:1-4), and even to employees and bosses (6:5-9), but he does so only *after* spending three chapters unpacking the gospel, *after* describing what Christian character looks like (4:1ff), *and* after the command in 5:18: "Be filled with (or controlled by) the Spirit." In short, if you try obeying Ephesians 5:22-6:9 withou submitting to the preceeding verses, you're toast.

Godly homes are comprised of godly people. *"Better ingredients, better pizza!"* You wa your marriage to improve? You want your relationship with your children to improve You want to be the start of a godly legacy? Begin by growing in grace yourself. There' no shortcut. Your walk with God "trickles down" to your relationships at home. Live a gospel-empowered life and your family will be "blessed" (Proverbs 20:7). That give you a huge responsibility. It also gives you a huge reason for hope.

Let the gospel shape your character and thereby bless your family. —CHRIS

Encouragement for the Discouraged
READ 2 CORINTHIANS 4

So we do not lose heart.
2 CORINTHIANS 4:16

s a Christian man, you are called to be a *minister for Christ*. Regardless of your gifts
r occupation, you are called to the advance the gospel and edify Christ's church.
Ve're all called to ministry, and ministry for Christ can be a discouraging endeavor.
1 2 Corinthians 4 Paul says twice, "We do not lose heart" (4:1, 16). In making such
atements he implies that faithful Christian ministry often involves discouragement.
hough we don't lose heart, we're frequently tempted to. The things that discouraged
aul are often the same things that discourage us. Ever have relationship problems
1 the church? Ever love Christians who didn't return that affection? Ever endure
·iticisms regarding your ministry abilities or integrity? Ministry is tough! Add to that
hysical trials, normal busyness, and financial pressure, and you have a perfect recipe
r *losing heart*. As discouragements compound, remembering four gospel-centered
uths from 2 Corinthians 4 will protect you from throwing in the towel.

Ministry for Christ is a privilege (4:1). The gospel you believe and advance is an
xceedingly glorious message. Read the previous chapter (ch. 3) and you'll see that
our ministry excels what Moses experienced at Sinai, where his face shone. How did
ou come to have this ministry? Simply by God's mercy (4:1). When you're weary in
inistry, recall that knowing the gospel, being in Christ's church, and ministering the
ospel to others are privileges.

Ministry is about Christ, not you (4:2-6). All Christian ministry involves rejection
nd apparent failure. In those times you're often tempted to tamper with the gospel
nessage itself (4:2). Why? Because you figure that softening the message will increase
our popularity. This reveals that your motives for ministry are self-aggrandizing.
Vhen you're weary in ministry, recall that ministry is about Christ, not you. Your
bors should be a straightforward exaltation of Christ, not an underhanded effort to
xalt yourself. If you'll forget yourself, God may use your undiluted gospel message to
pen eyes that are blind to the glory of Christ (4:3-6).

Ministry for Christ will look like the cross (4:7-15). Paul compares you to a clay
ot (4:7). His point is that you're common, not impressive. The more you look and
el like a clay pot, the more people will pay attention to your message rather than
ou. As God allows things to afflict you, perplex you, persecute you, and strike you
own (4:8-9), what He's doing is conforming you to the crucifixion of Christ (4:10-
5)—an unimpressive death that resulted in a fruitful resurrection. When you're weary,
emember that your ministry is supposed to look like your message: power in weakness.

Ministry for Christ has a good end (4:16-18). Take heart. Whatever ministry is
killing you"—making your outer nature waste away (4:16)—is not permanent. And
1e reward will far outweigh the pain (4:17). "It will be worth it all when we see Jesus,"
s Esther Rusthoi's hymn encourages us.

.re you prone to discouragement because of the hardships in your ministry for Christ?
in the club. Ever since the days of Paul, faithful Christians in normal churches have
truggled with discouragement. To keep going, remember that ministry is a privilege,
1at ministry is about Christ, that ministry will look like the cross, and that the
ardships of ministry won't last forever.

et the gospel encourage you during hard times of ministry. —JOE

Gospel-Controlled Sexuality
READ 1 CORINTHIANS 6

You are not your own, for you were bought with a price.
So glorify God in your body.
1 CORINTHIANS 6:19-20

A very basic reading of the New Testament reveals that the gospel is as crucial for Christians as for non-Christians. When Christians are proud, Paul applies the gospel to them (1 Corinthians 1-4); when Christians are legalistic, Paul again preaches the gospel to them (Galatians); when Christians are tempted to live in sin, Paul explores the implications of the cross and resurrection (Romans 6). What do you expect Paul to do when Christians are immoral? Surprise! He applies the gospel to them.

How does the gospel affect your sexuality? What does your union with Jesus' death and resurrection have to do with who you sleep with?" 1 Corinthians 6:12-20 is one of the clearest texts about how the gospel relates to our sexuality. In the passage, Paul gives two commands ("flee immorality" and "glorify God in your body") that are rooted in four gospel arguments. It's these four gospel arguments that we're going to unpack here.

Your body will be raised (6:14). This single-verse preview of 1 Corinthians 15 hints at the vast implications of our bodily resurrection. When you believed in Jesus, you were united with Jesus' work—with His death, burial, *and resurrection*. Because Jesus rose bodily from the grave, you will, too. That means that what you do with your body matters! The gospel should change the way you view your body.

Your body is united with Jesus (6:15-18). You are united, not only with Jesus' work, but also with Jesus Himself. "Your bodies are members of Christ" (6:15). And if, as Paul argues, sexual intercourse expresses a physical oneness with one's sexual partner (6:16), then how wicked is it for you—a man whose body is united with Christ—to use your body for immorality? Your union with Christ should be a controlling factor in your sexual behavior.

Your body is a temple of the Holy Spirit (6:18-19). Paul's third argument for sexual purity is this: the Holy Spirit indwells every believer's body (Ephesians 1:13-14; Romans 8:9-10). The inevitable effects of the gospel include the Spirit's indwelling. Your body is the Holy Spirit's temple. Therefore, don't trash God's temple.

Your body belongs to God (6:19-20). Through the redeeming work of Jesus, God purchased your body. He purchased *you*. He didn't merely pay the price to free you from your bondage to sin; He paid for *you*. Jesus owns you—body and all! This means that if you sin sexually, you're abusing something that doesn't belong to you; you're damaging Jesus' property—property which He bought at the cost of His life.

Did you notice how each of these four arguments is rooted in the basics of the gospel? Right thinking about the gospel has everything to do with how you live. The gospel is life-changing, not just soul-saving. The primary reason so many Christian men fall to sexual temptation so consistently, whether physically or mentally, is that they have not applied the gospel deeply enough.

Let the gospel control your sexuality. —JOE

The Gospel Precludes Prejudice

READ JOHN 3-4

We have heard for ourselves,
and we know that this is indeed the Savior of the world.
JOHN 4:42

The Gospel of John overflows with Christ's words. He debated religious hypocrites. He taught the disciples. He prayed to His Father. He also dialogued with individual sinners. In particular, His conversations with Nicodemus (John 3) and "the bad Samaritan" (John 4) provide a striking display of the universality of the gospel, highlighting our need for salvation and dealing a deathblow to our prejudice.

In John 3, Jesus had a famous nighttime interview with Nicodemus. Nicodemus was the epitome of respectability (3:1). He was a man. He was a Jew. He was a Pharisee. He was a ruler, a member of the Sanhedrin (the Jewish supreme court). He was a great teacher—literally *the* teacher in Israel (3:10). Yet, he was lost. Unimpressed by Nick's spiritual résumé, Jesus told him that he needed to be born again (3:3).

Move ahead to chapter 4. Here Jesus met with the anti-Nicodemus, one of the most pathetic characters in the Scriptures. The woman Jesus engaged by a well on a hot day was despised, not respected. She was a lowly Samaritan—a half-breed—not a Jew (4:7). She had been repeatedly disappointed and immoral, married five times and now shacked up with another man (4:16-18). She couldn't be more different from our Pharisee friend. The disciples were shocked that Jesus would speak with her (4:27), as was she (4:9)! In contrast, no one would have raised an eyebrow about Jesus' conversation with Nicodemus (which took place in secret).

Yet, Christ treated these two poles of humanity in precisely the same way. In both cases He used an outward illustration to show an inward need. Nicodemus needed spiritual birth, not just physical (3:5-7). The Samaritan woman needed satisfaction of her spiritual thirst, not just physical (4:13-15). In both cases, Jesus pointed to faith in Himself as the only means of salvation, showing the universal need of the gospel, the universal appeal of the gospel, and the universal offer of the gospel. He saved a supposedly holy man, and He saved a notoriously lowly woman, thereby reaching an entire village of sinners (4:39-42). The rescue of one harlot resulted in a great harvest (4:35). The gospel does that. It's contagious.

At the conclusion of the John 4 narrative, the newly converted Samaritans marveled that Jesus is "the Savior *of the world*" (4:42). That's not a random statement. John highlights for us the fact that Christ doesn't just save Jews, the religious and respectable. There is no favoritism with God. Though the Samaritans were "from the other side of the tracks," they were welcomed by Christ. A Pharisee and a divorcee were made equal by their sin and their Savior. Sinners are united and divisions obliterated by the gospel (Colossians 1:27; 3:11). To quote missionary J. D. Crowley, "The gospel drives a cross-shaped dagger into the heart of racism."

Right between these two great narratives in the book of John is a dividing line that separates all people into two groups. John 3:36 divides all humanity in two: those *who have trusted Christ* and are thus saved from their sin, and those *who have not trusted Christ* and are thus damned for their sin. Be sure you've been saved from God's wrath by faith in Christ. Then rejoice that you're part of Christ's church, where sinners from various cultures and classes are united and where prejudice dies.

Let the gospel inspire your love for the multi-ethnic body of Christ! —CHRIS

Security & Assurance

READ ROMANS 8

All who are led by the Spirit of God are sons of God.
ROMANS 8:14

Romans 8 is all about security. It opens with the words, "There is…no condemnation for those who are in Christ Jesus" (8:1). It ends with the words, "[Nothing] will be able to separate us from the love of God in Christ Jesus our Lord" (8:39). We are secure in Christ! Why, then, do we often doubt our security? For several reasons. First, we can lack assurance because our indwelling sin is still alive and well (8:1-14). Second, we can doubt our security because we're experiencing the effects of the Fall (8:10, 20-23). Sometimes our groaning is so deep that we don't even know how to talk to God (8:26). Third, fears of condemnation can cause us to doubt our security (8:31-34). Due to our past and present sins, we can carry with us lurking suspicions: "When I stand before God, will He really not remember my sins against me? Will He really accept me as holy?" Finally, persecution can leave us feeling like God has abandoned us (8:35-39).

Thankfully, our security in Christ is *objective*; though our assurance (our sense of security) is *subjective*. When you're on a rollercoaster that's been professionally designed, built, and approved, are you secure? Yes. As you ride it, do you *feel* secure? Not likely. Our security in Christ isn't based on our feelings of security, but on what God has done for us in Christ. In this chapter, Paul teaches us that our assurance—our experience of security—comes from the Holy Spirit's personal application of Christ's work.

We have "the Spirit of life" (8:1-11). The Spirit of God has applied Christ's sacrifice to every Christian, setting us free from condemnation (8:1-3). He has given us a mind that, like Christ's, is set on serving God and others (8:4-8). This Spirit that indwells us is the same Spirit who raised Jesus to life from the dead (8:9-11). Christ rose from the dead; the Holy Spirit works that resurrection power within us.

We have "the Spirit of adoption" (8:12-17). The Spirit moves us from condemnation to sonship. Being led by the Spirit to kill sin is a sure mark of our adoption into God's family (8:12-14). He also assures us that we are God's sons by leading us to cry with childlike intimacy to God our Father (8:15-17). Christ's work makes our adoption possible; the Spirit makes us look and feel like God's children.

We have "the firstfruits of the Spirit" (8:18-25). Even though we groan with all of creation (8:18-22), we groan in hope (8:23-25), knowing that our present experience of the Holy Spirit is just the tip of the iceberg of our eternal blessings. Christ has redeemed us; the Spirit's work in us is a foretaste of the glorious day when that redemption will be fully realized.

We have the Spirit who "intercedes for us" (Romans 8:26-30). The Spirit perfectly knows God's purpose for us: that we "be conformed to the image of His Son" (8:28-30). He knows that's a process that must include suffering (which means that suffering is productive, not random). He also knows it's a process that's as good as done from God's perspective. In other words, the Spirit knows exactly how to pray for us when we're going through hard times (8:26-27)! Because of Christ's work, one day we'll be glorified; and until that process is done, the Spirit will keep interceding for us.

In Christ we're secure; through the Spirit, we're sure of it. Do you hate your sin? Do you instinctively cry to God, your Father? Does suffering make you long to see Jesus? If so, rejoice that the Spirit is working in you to assure you that you're God's child.

Let the gospel silence your doubts. —JOE

Barnabas-Like Ministry

READ ACTS 4:34–37 & 11:19–30

When he came and saw the grace of God, he was glad,
and he exhorted them all to remain faithful to the Lord.

ACTS 11:23

One of my heroes is Barnabas. He's the kind of guy that can easily go unnoticed, but he was a remarkable man. I've prayed many times for "a church of Barnabai" (my own grammatically-indefensible plural form). What would that look like?

Barnabas was a godly servant. We're first introduced to noble Barnabas in Acts 4:34-37. He's not preaching or performing miracles. He's just selling part of his property and giving the proceeds to the apostles in order to help with benevolence needs within the infant church. We also learn that he was a native of Cyprus and that his real name was Joseph. "Barnabas" was his nickname, given to him by the apostles. It's a telling name, for it means "son of encouragement." I love that. Barnabas is a man who oozed gospel grace—the same grace that had shaped his own character (11:24).

Barnabas was a selfless mentor. The next time we encounter Barnabas, he's again encouraging others. This time the recipient is an unlikely convert to Christianity named Saul of Tarsus (Acts 9:26-28). Perhaps you've heard of him? The man who had been the church's greatest adversary would become its greatest advocate, but not without a mentor who put his neck on the line and gave him a vote of confidence.

Barnabas disappears from the pages of Acts for about a decade before surfacing again in Acts 11:19-26. The gospel had expanded from Jerusalem to Antioch, about 300 miles to the north. The church at Antioch was an "outside-the-box church," planted among non-Jews (11:20) and led in time by men of various colors and classes (Acts 13:1). Such an upstart church needed just the right man to mentor its members. Perhaps the choice was as obvious to the church at Jerusalem as it is to me, because they sent Barnabas. I love the report of his ministry there in Acts 11:23. His ministry in Antioch exploded, and in typical form, he pulled Saul (now Paul) into ministry with him (11:25-26). Was Barnabas' ministry in Antioch effective? More than we'll ever really know, I think. The body adopted the heartbeat of its pastor: it reached out like him (11:24b), gave like him (11:27-30), and had godly character like him. Whereas Joseph had been aptly called Barnabas, the church he led was called by a more striking name: "Christians" (11:26).

Barnabas was an audacious evangelist. Based on the depth of Barnabas' ministry at Antioch, you'd think the church would be utterly dependent on him and Paul. Not so. When the Lord called Pastors Barnabas and Paul to go out from Antioch to take the gospel to unreached cities throughout Asia, the church at Antioch did fine (Acts 13). Their mentor had taught them to cling to Christ, not him, and thus they survived his departure (2 Timothy 2:2). Indeed, the church at Antioch became the leading church of its day, the "spiritual slingshot" that would send missionaries around the known world. You can read of Paul and Barnabas' exploits as church planting missionary pioneers in Acts 13-15. It's an amazing read. It speaks of courage amidst opposition, of humble cooperation among gifted men, of bold risk-taking for gospel advancement, of determined defense of the purity of the gospel, and mostly of relentless passion to see the glory of God spread among the unreached.

Let the gospel transform you into a grace-spreading mentor. —CHRIS

"Get Mark"

READ ACTS 13:1–13 & 15:36–41

Get Mark and bring him with you, for he is very useful to me for ministry.
2 TIMOTHY 4:11

Yesterday we considered the legacy of Barnabas, the servant-mentor-evangelist. He helped the Apostle Paul get started in the ministry, and he founded the church at Antioch. That's a pretty good epitaph, but there's more. Barnabas had a sister named Mary. We don't know a great deal about her, but we learn in Acts 12:12 that the church in Jerusalem met in her home. She had a son named John Mark. He had been born into a family of spiritual privilege. He may have known Jesus during His earthly ministry. He certainly knew most of the apostles and was a convert of the Apostle Peter (1 Peter 5:13). When his Uncle Barnabas and Paul went out from Antioch on the first missionary journey, he went along as their assistant (Acts 12:25; 13:5).

Unfortunately, a good start doesn't guarantee success. Just as the first mission trip was getting going, he quit. Acts 13:13 gives us a rather hasty record of his departure: "John left them and returned to Jerusalem." We're not told the reason, but it certainly wasn't good. Paul took it as a spiritual mutiny (Acts 15:38). The team went on without him and had tremendous success. But John Mark's legacy would apparently be failure.

Three or four years passed. Paul and Barnabas prepared for another trip. Barnabas, ever the encourager, wanted to give John Mark a second chance. Paul refused. The conflict between them was severe, though probably not sinful. They split. Paul took Silas on the originally planned mission trip. Barnabas took John Mark and went to Cyprus (Acts 15:36–41). Barnabas disappears from the book of Acts, which instead follows Paul.

End of story? Hardly. It's just getting good. Fast forward about twelve years. Paul is in prison, writing a letter to the church at Colossae. As he draws the letter to a close, he mentions a number of his companions. Read Colossians 4:10. Paul makes mention of "Mark the cousin of Barnabas." We know that guy! He's the one who started like a rocket and ended like a rock. But Paul (of all people!) calls him a "fellow worker" and "comfort" (4:11). He urges the church at Colossae to receive John Mark—perhaps an indication that Mark was still trying to overcome his reputation. Now, jump ahead another eight years. Paul's in prison again, this time for the last time. He's writing another letter, this time to Timothy. Again he closes the letter with some personal allusions, and again he speaks of John Mark. This time, however, he's not *sending* him as he did in Colossians 4:10; he's *requesting* him. My eyes fill with tears just to think it. The aged apostle is nearing his own death, and he asks Timothy to bring John Mark, the kid he'd written off some twenty years before. "Get Mark and bring him with you, for he is very useful to me for ministry" (2 Timothy 4:11). Don't you just love grace? But we're still not quite at the end of the story. According to church history, John Mark worked alongside Peter. He founded and pastored a strong church in Alexandria, Egypt. He eventually laid down his life as a martyr, but not before leaving us his most enduring legacy (and perhaps the most enduring legacy of his Uncle Barnabas): the biblical gospel of Mark. "Very useful," indeed.

My brothers, be encouraged by God's gracious restoring of a notorious failure. God delights to fix what seems irreparably broken. Failure need not be final. Remember that as you look at your own life. Remember it as you look at the apparently ruined lives around you. And pray that the Lord will use you to salvage lives that appear to be wasted but can still be "very useful" in our Lord's service.

Let the gospel restore you and others as trophies of salvaging grace. —CHRIS

Are You in the Will of God?

READ ECCLESIASTES 11–12

This Jesus, delivered up according to the definite plan
and foreknowledge of God, you...killed by the hands of lawless men.

ACTS 2:23

What is the will of God? How do we know the will of God? Am I in the will of God? These are huge, hard questions. Many Christian men are confused about how to answer them. How do I know? Because I hear many Christians say things like, "I got out of God's will a few years back, and I'll never be able to get back in." "I need to know what God's will is before I decide which job to take." Statements like these are spiritually suffocating, and worse, unbiblical.

The most basic, pastorally-helpful advice I can give you regarding God's will is this: you must recognize that *the will of God* can refer to two different things: God's *sovereign* will and God's *moral* will. Throughout history, Bible-reading Christians have understood that there is a difference between what God has determined and what He desires, between what God wills to happen and what He wants to happen, between what God decrees and what He commands. Let me give three examples of the difference between "God's will" and "God's will."

Is it God's will that all people be saved? That's a trick question. Does God desire that all people be saved? Absolutely! The Lord "desires all people to be saved and to come to the knowledge of the truth" (1 Timothy 2:4). Yet, has God willed that every human be saved? Clearly not, or else they would be (John 1:12-13).

Was David's adultery with Bathsheba God's will? God forbid! David broke every command in the book! He idolized pleasure, coveted his neighbor's wife, committed adultery, lied, and committed murder. Clearly, this was not God's will. Yet David also penned one of my favorite verses: "Your eyes saw my unformed substance; in your book were written, every one of them, the days that were formed for me, when as yet there were none of them" (Psalm 139:16). Could David really look at every day of his life (colossal failures and all) and be certain that it was all planned out by His loving Creator before he ever lived one day of it? Yes.

Was it God's will that men kill His innocent Son out of murderous envy? Your wrestlings with God's will should always end up at Calvary. The cross was the most heinous crime in human history and yet—at the same time—in perfect keeping with God's eternal will (Acts 2:23; 4:28; 5:38). So was Christ's death the result of the decree of God or the sin of Pilate, Herod, and other men? Well, *yes*.

What does this mean for the way you think about your life and your decisions? It means that when you look at your past, you have to recognize that every time you've not done God's moral will (and every time someone has not done God's will toward you), it's still all within God's sovereign will for your life. It also means that, when you make decisions, you don't need to know God's sovereign will—His grand design. You don't need to "be God" in decision-making. God will surely frustrate you in that pursuit (Ecclesiastes 11:5). Instead, you need to study the Word, seek wise advice, pray, and evaluate your gifts, opportunities, and desires. You need to trust God, take responsibility, and take some risks in the confidence that you cannot escape God's sovereign will for your life (Proverbs 16:9).

Let the gospel strengthen your confidence in God's sovereign will and your commitment to His moral will. —JOE

The Survival Guide for Sinners
READ 1 JOHN 1-2

But if anyone does sin, we have an advocate with the Father,
Jesus Christ the righteous.

1 JOHN 2:1

I hate sin. Except for when I love it. You know the cycle: you genuinely detest sin for what it cost your Savior, yet you sometimes crave it. And when you yield to it, you h. it all the more. Our relationship to sin is complicated. That's why I end with what ha become my favorite text of Scripture: 1 John 2:1-2, The Survival Guide for Sinners.

Plan A: Run to Christ, and don't sin. 1 John 2:1 records God's will for the Christian The aged Apostle John tells his readers that he's written to them so they'll stop sinnin That's God's desire. That's our desire, if we're saved. We've been released from sin's po by Christ's death and resurrection. Our heart toward it has changed. We fight it. So John says, "Don't sin." Awesome. I agree. Now let's bow in prayer and be done with i

If only it were that easy! The problem is, we *do* sin. John just finished saying that if w say we haven't sinned or don't sin, we're lying (1:8-10). I'm not telling you to shrug o sin or plan for it. But I am telling you to *expect* it. You'll still lose your temper as you' growing in patience. You'll still have sinful thoughts as you're growing in purity. You' still struggle with laziness, or gluttony, or arrogance, or harshness, or selfishness, or whatever your particular besetting sins are. It's not okay; Scripture commands you to stop. Fight your sin. Resist temptation. But what about when you *do* blow it—*again?*

Plan B: When you sin, run to Christ. How grateful I am that 1 John 2:1 doesn't end with the command not to sin. Keep reading and you'll get to the "Survival Guide" pa If (when) you sin, don't despair. God has made provision for you. "We have an advoc with the Father, Jesus Christ the righteous." Jesus is the sinner's Defense Attorney. He pleads for us when Satan accuses us (justly) of sin. The Lord Jesus Himself appears before His Father to make intercession for us (Hebrews 7:25; 9:24).

Think further about this. If Jesus argues our case when we sin, what exactly does He argue? He can't claim that we're innocent, because we're not. He doesn't look for a lega loophole, like some celebrity attorney. So what does He say? That's where 1 John 2:2 comes in. Jesus argues that our crimes have been paid for. He's not only "the righteous One," Whose obedience is imputed to us. He's also "the propitiation for our sins," Wł has had our disobedience imputed to Him. *Propitiation* means that Christ has entirely satisfied God's wrath on our sin—not by avoiding it or deflecting it, but by *absorbing* To use the imagery Jesus invoked in the Garden of Gethsemane, Christ drank the dreg of God's wrath against sin. He emptied the cup (Matthew 26:39; John 18:11). God is appeased. So when we sin, we run to Christ, our Advocate and Propitiation.

I run to Christ when stalked by sin, And find a sure escape;
"Deliver me!" I cry to Him; temptation yields to grace.
I run to Christ when plagued by shame, And find my one Defense;
"I bore God's wrath," He pleads my case, My Advocate and Friend.

One of the greatest delights of heaven will be the absence of sin. How wonderful to be free from temptation, free from my flesh, and "saved to sin no more" (William Cowper). Amen. Come, Lord Jesus! But in the meantime, even as I labor to apply th gospel to avoid sin, my great hope isn't my perfect obedience, heartfelt confessions, o intentions to do better next time. My hope is Christ. I've got nothing else.

Let the gospel restrain you from sinning and restore you when you do. —CHRIS